REVENUE SUPERSTAR!

THE SIMPLE RULES OF HOTEL REVENUE MANAGEMENT

Johan Hammer

Johan@revenuesuperstar.com
Instagram: revenuesuperstar

ISBN 978-91-639-1680-9

Contents

What this book covers

This book contains 13 frequently asked questions about hotel revenue management.

This book will cover many topics, including:

Forecasting
Efficiency
Daily tasks
Rate setting
Promotions
Budgets
Distribution
Trends
Creativity
Programmatic advertising
Social proof
Math
Prospect Theory
Paretos Principle
The power of inversion
Wholesale
Group rate setting
Non-pricing
Yielding
CRM & Big Data

Before we begin. Make sure to sign up for my newsletter. Be the first one to know when there is news updates or special promotions www.revenuesuperstar.com/newsletter

As you are reading, please refer to the glossary of terms if you encounter any industry lingo for which you are unfamiliar with as it pertains to hotel revenue management.

Introduction

"History reports that the men who can manage men manage the men who can manage only things, and the men who can manage money manage all."

— Will Durant, *The Lessons of History*

I once read that out of all of the professions in the world, hospitality revenue managers have worked with the greatest number of different systems over the last ten to fifteen years. At a time when all others industries were already relying upon fancy interfaces under which all their systems were consolidated, we still had to manage ten to fifteen different extranets every single day. A big shout-out to all of you who managed to survive! Luckily, today's systems are at last more in line with those in other industries.

Charles Darwin once said, "It is not the strongest of the species that survives, nor the most intelligent that survives. It is the one that is most adaptable to change."

Being the most adaptable to change holds true to what I will convey throughout this book. The revenue management profession is constantly changing and within the next ten to fifteen years will blend together with many other professions, even more so than it already does now. We will see a new commercial revenue specialist evolve who can manage multiple hotels from a strategic commercial level.

The new commercial specialists will be able to oversee and manage systems using data from all possible sources, including E-commerce, advertising, customer reputation management, business intelligence, reservation statistics, airlines, demographic trends, and much more. Smart systems like these are already here, but their user interfaces will continue to evolve further over the next five to ten years. We will soon reach a point where these smart systems are as customizable as our smartphones.

As R. "RAY" Wang so wisely stated it in his book, *Disrupting Digital Business*, "These next-generation platforms are changing the way we look at technologies. But we can't throw away the existing technologies. They're there, but we build layers into each one of them... The final layer is mass personalization at scale, and that is where we are going... To be able to move there as a brand or individual, we must first ask the right questions instead of seeking the right answers."

In this book, you will find what I believe to be timeless principles that will continue to be true even as our industry marches along its ever-evolving path. It does not matter whether you are already an experienced revenue manager, just starting out, or someone who just wants to learn more about the profession; regardless of what stage of your revenue management career you are at, you will find valuable, practical ideas in this book that will help you thrive.

Keep on rocking, guys!

A brief overview of Revenue Management

Sell the right room to the right customer at the right time through the right channel. Or as my previous mentor, Pontus Mark, so wisely put it:

> "Sell the room to the one who needs it the most."

As an hotelier, we are in a business that sells a service, but providing this service has a challenging constraint attached to it. We must sell the room before it disappears. We can never start a winter sale or sell our rooms the day *after* an arrival date has passed. To make providing this service even trickier, we also have to deal with fixed capacity and demand variations in the forms of seasons, multiple competitors, and a very crowded web space.

However, it is not enough to just fill our rooms. Rooms must be filled with the correct mix of segments producing the best possible bottom-line profit for the hotel. As a revenue manager, you have to factor in distribution channels, average length of stays, variable pricing, lead-times, commission levels, online reputation, historical data, data quality, segments, and the list goes on and on. But don't worry, we revenue managers tend to make it sound more difficult than it is.

To make things simpler, I have compiled a list of the 13 most frequently asked questions I receive regarding Revenue Management. This is a list of questions, along with *around* 37 possible answers, that I wish I had had to reference when I started out as a revenue manager. Not just knowing the answers, but knowing the right questions to ask in the first place would have made my life much, much easier.

(Before we get started asking and answering the questions on my list, note that if you would like to know more about the history of Revenue Management, I suggest just Googling it. I am not going to bore you with my longwinded account of its history here.)

About the author

In his book *Outliers*, Malcolm Gladwell states that it takes roughly ten thousand hours of practice to achieve mastery in one's given field. I long ago surpassed my ten thousand hours as a hospitality professional, but I continue improving upon my mastery daily.

I started my career as a bellhop parking fancy cars at a five-star hotel in the heart of Copenhagen. Within five years, I had managed to fight my way through the system to launch my new career as a Revenue Manager responsible for looking after online distribution for eighteen Hotels in Denmark. The brand I work for is called First Hotels.

Though already a revenue manager, I continue to educate myself so that I can continue to perform my job even better. To this end, in 2015, I earned a certificate from Cornell University after completing their course titled: *Advanced Hospitality Revenue Management: Pricing and Demand Strategies.*

As of the writing of this book in 2016, I still work for First Hotels under the title of Revenue & Distribution Specialist. My main role is to consult with our hotels regarding revenue- and distribution-related matters. I also internally analyze and suggest new strategies for the brand and its stakeholders.

As far as my working practice is concerned, I have a strange desire to put myself into complicated situations in order to figure out the best solutions. Once I find a solution, I like to simplify it and package it so others can more easily understand it.

As Einstein so elegantly put it:

> *"Everything should be made as simple as possible but not simpler."*

I am truly grateful that my current employer has given me so much freedom to experiment, learn, and pivot throughout my ten years working for First Hotels. I would not have been able to share these simple rules of revenue management with you without such freedom, nor would this book have ever been possible.

In short, what inspired me to write this book was my frustration at not being able to find a simple book that explains revenue management in a way that anybody can understand.

2017 update:

Most recently, in June 2017, I co-founded a travel startup called Instaroom.travel where we build cool messaging technology to help hotels digitalize guest conversations and convert complicated bookings directly on their own websites. Our technology is 100% AI ready, which means it contains many smart tools and the ability to automate most conversations. The hotel website is the most visited department in a hotel, and currently it's unstaffed. The first step a hotel should take is to put a messaging widget on their website. Messaging is here to stay. After all, research shows that at least 88% of people born after 1981 prefer communicating via messaging.

Feel free to reach out to me at johan@instaroom.travel to learn more and to get a free trial of Instaroom for your hotel or brand. www.instaroom.travel

Daily pricing decisions, what should I look for?

The decisions you make regarding daily pricing vary significantly from day to day. It can be rather daunting to know where to begin. Here are some tactics I rely upon over and over again to help me make my own decisions easily.

Pickup trends

Do not adjust your pricing and restrictions based on the pickup number. We need to know what is driving the pickup in order to see if we need to make any adjustments.

Ask yourself, what was booked yesterday? How did it affect the business we already had?

You might want to think twice before raising your rate if you know that you only had pickup in segments with static rates. In this situation, raising your dynamic rates might depress the pickup on your higher yielding rates, including these dynamic rates, entirely.

Is your pickup filling up too quickly from lower paying segments? If so, consider setting up some restrictions. A couple of times a week you should probably ask yourself what will be going on 4 to 12 months into the future. In particular, while looking ahead, try to identify new trends or trends that are repeating themselves.

Market and competitors

It is also important to keep an eye on what your competitors are doing. Watching your competitors will let you know when good opportunities exist to increase rates and help you identify trends before you might have otherwise. If you do not already have a tool to track this kind of information, the major OTAs, at the very least, offer free ones, which is better than nothing. Rate Intelligence from Booking.com is just one example.

I have tested many different tools for "Competitive Rate intelligence", and the best one I have encountered so far is OTA Insight (www.otainsight.com). This site offers a very simple tool with a clean user interface. It also provides very accurate demand forecasts for the near future. I always say that once you find a tool even a general manager likes and wants to use, then you know that you've found the right one. OTA Insight is the first such tool I have found that matches this criterion.

Inventory control

Make sure your room inventory is always balanced.

In other words, make sure you have rooms available when they need to be available. If you sold out of your most popular room type, you might want to upgrade or set up overbooking rules in order to not miss good opportunities such as long stayers and last-minute premium rate bookers.

If, for example, your standard room category sells out for a Tuesday, you might miss out on guests who have agreements only for that particular room type, but who want to stay several nights in addition to Tuesday.

Lead time trends

Can history and ongoing trends help you identify opportunities to optimize specific "segmented lead-times"?

Let me give you an example of what I mean: When going over the results from the latest high season you notice that double room reservations made from the US had a booking window that was 30 days longer than domestic reservations.

Suppose this US business is good because they tend to stay longer and spend more money at the hotel; in that case, you would probably want to leverage this opportunity next year or during another similar period to make sure you attract even more of this traffic. Preferably, you also want to do this via direct channels that normally have lower distribution costs.

This is normally something you should practice every month when doing your monthly business review. Once a year consolidate your findings, and convert them into practical action points in your budget and forecast process. On a daily basis, the best practice would be to try to catch ongoing trends and build a mental framework of what to look for when you conduct your monthly business review. If you find some ongoing trends, you might be able to replicate them for the short term. Try setting up some experiments to see how you can stimulate more of this good business.

Looking for a daily checklist? Go here to download the free Revenue Superstar Daily checklist. It's a simple checklist you can use daily to make sure you get the most important things done first. www.revenuesuperstar.com/the-revenue-superstar-daily-checklist

Recommendation

If you are looking for a simple revenue management system to replace your old pickup and pace spreadsheets, then you should have a look at systems such as Pace, Atomize or Juyo Analytics. Use the systems to set up automatic or semi-automatic pricing structures which will free up time and increase revenues.

The systems are also extremely user friendly :)

Do I need to be a math genius to be a revenue manager?

"Meeting complexity with complexity can create more confusion than it resolves."

— Donald Sull

No, you don't need to be a math genius, but you do need to know how to calculate percentages and ratios. When it comes to calculating percentages, it is unbelievable to see how often people get this wrong.

Here is an example. Let's say one of your distribution partners asks you for 20% off your retail rates because they have a margin they must stick to in order to turn a profit themselves. Their margins might already be reduced by market fees or because the third parties with whom they work will also take their share of the pie. The argument this partner makes is that they need to add 20% to turn a profit; therefore, they request 20% off your retail rates.

Adding 20%, though, is not the same as removing 20%. If you take 20% away from 100, you get 80. But if you add 20% to 80, you only get 96. This is very basic, but I believe basics are king; people too often underestimate them because the basics are so simple. If a partner needs to add 20% to a net rate, your best bet is to only reduce your rates between 16 and 17% (16,67% to be precise).

You should think about taxes the same way. If the tax percentage is 20%, it's always 20% added to the net, not 20% removed from the gross.

When it comes to ratios, this is also important, because you need to be able to calculate your returns on your investments. Take, for example, determining what a specific campaign will bring in. If you're making a marketing effort, you have costs involved, thus you must be able to predict that those costs will produce a certain ratio of outcome and revenues to justify them. You need to understand ratios to ensure that you provide a return on investment to the stakeholders, the hotel manager, and the brand.

Learn percentages and ratios. Specifically, learn what the difference is between adding percentages versus removing them. Once you have successfully added calculating percentages and ratios to your tool belt, you can then begin building upon these basics to grow increasingly strategic about how you manage and increase your revenue.

PERCENTAGE EXAMPLE

VALUE	%	EQUALS
$1000	-30%	$700
$ 700	+30%	$910

From a revenue management perspective, where should my daily focus reside?

"Being busy is not the same as being productive. In fact, being busy is a form of laziness—lazy thinking and indiscriminate action"

– Tim Ferriss

I believe this is the same for everybody. You must focus on what brings you and your company the most value.

The Rule of 3

This is the most important—yet the simplest—rule for daily effectiveness: Every day you should have a list of the three things you want to accomplish that day. Preferably, you should create this list the day prior to allow your brain to start planning and working on these tasks, even if only in the background.

You will probably say: "That's crazy, I have many more things to accomplish in a day than just three. Why shouldn't I put more things on my list?"

You will always have more than three things on your list, but the importance of these three things transcends the things that otherwise comprise your daily routine. These are things that if you do not do anything else throughout your entire day, you will still feel productive if you accomplish them. The few very important things you do in a day often represent most of the value that all your tasks combined achieve. (More about this below when I explain the Pareto Principle.)

Examples you might include on your list of three things are:

- Call Expedia and finish winter promotion set up
- Collect data to prepare BAR setting analysis
- Sign all contracts in my to-do folder
- Create power point template for revenue meeting
- Call hotel manager to discuss yesterday's email
- Conduct business review of the previous month
- Prepare for meeting with sales and marketing departments
- Create a six-month forecast
- Prepare introduction for new colleague

I borrowed this rule from Chris Bailey after reading his book *The Productivity Project* and have relied upon it ever since. I highly recommend this book if you are looking for even more ways to improve your productivity and effectiveness. In Bailey's own words, though:

"The absolute best technique I've found to work deliberately and with intention every day is the Rule of 3."

While you can go buy this book and learn a lot of awesome stuff, the point to remember here is that you must manage your own time or somebody else will.

The Pareto Principle

The Pareto Principle derives its name from Vilfredo Pareto, the economist who first discerned the principle's existence. The principle explains how an unequal relationship exists between inputs and outputs, wherein for many phenomena, 20% of invested inputs are responsible for 80% of the results obtained. This is known as the 80/20 rule.

A simple example of the 80/20 rule: Which 20% of your hotel's distribution channels stands for 80% of the reservations? This is where to focus time and money when setting up campaigns or promotions. Do not focus on the trivial many; instead, focus on the vital few.

I also believe this holds true throughout the day of a revenue manager.

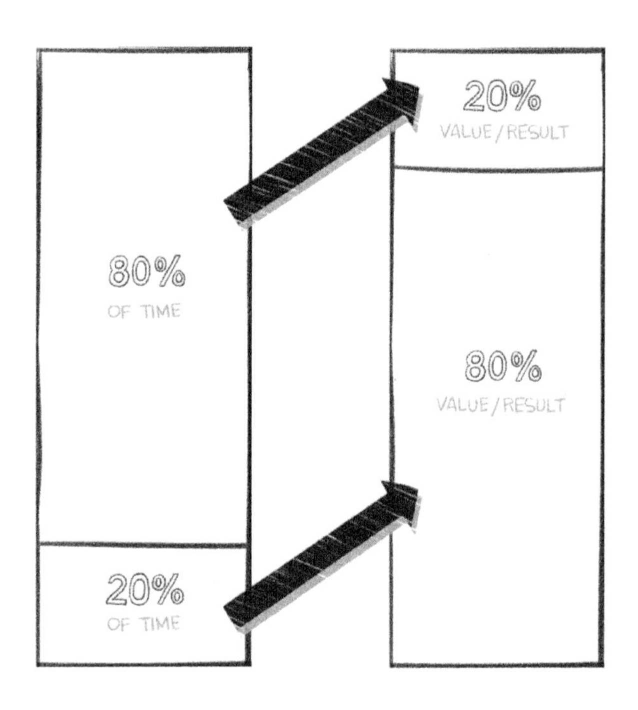

How to structure each day as a revenue manager

First, I recommend that you try to make your reoccurring daily tasks as automatic as possible. This requires teaching yourself systems that allow you to eventually perform as many tasks as possible without needing to give them second thoughts. For example, many property management systems allow for automatic rate restriction rules. Learn how to establish these rules; because they are automatic, once you set them up, you no longer have to think about them, thus freeing your mind to devote your attentions to other, more complicated tasks. **Looking for a daily checklist?** Go here to download the free Revenue Superstar Daily checklist. It's a simple checklist you can use daily to make sure you get the most important things done first. www.revenuesuperstar.com/the-revenue-superstar-daily-checklist

A second recommendation I can offer to you is to remove as many distractions as possible. If you receive several daily reports, decide which must be reviewed on a daily basis and which can wait to be reviewed weekly or even monthly. You will eventually learn to trust your instincts on this matter, knowing which reports can wait and which cannot. The result will be you no longer waste time reviewing less essential reports more often than you need to; you'll have a solid schedule that you stick to because it proves effective.

Third, let me share with you how I set up my day daily, so you in turn can model your day based on it and the specific needs of your revenue management practice. I have developed this setup after many years spent testing different approaches. I find this setup to make the most efficient use of my time:

1. Complete daily pricing activities. Open/Close and Change rates (60 min). (This is also known as Yield Management.)

   Note: I do not open my mailbox until I complete this activity!

2. Perform other very important daily activities, such as group quotations and large revenue generating tasks (60 min).

   Be sure to group *like* tasks together to avoid wasting time. Examples include:
   - Making phone calls
   - Performing tasks that require the same computer system
   - Soliciting corporate RFPs and other requests for proposals
   - Writing emails to the same person
   - Signing contracts
   - Printing documents

3. The Rule of 3 (180 min).

   As you can see, I devote the most amount of time to the three most important tasks that I must complete in a given day.

4. Emails (60 min). This, sadly, is where most people start...

5. Prioritize and Plan (60 min).

   - Plan tomorrow. For example, write the next day's Rule of 3.

- Identify bottlenecks. What did not go as planned today? Take action to change whatever it was that derailed you plan from derailing it in the future. For examples: set up new procedures, create a SOP, etc.

6. Other (60 min).

   This is your cushion. It allows you to deal with the unexpected, write more emails or, when everything goes right and you're all caught up, go have ice cream :)

Total: 8 hours

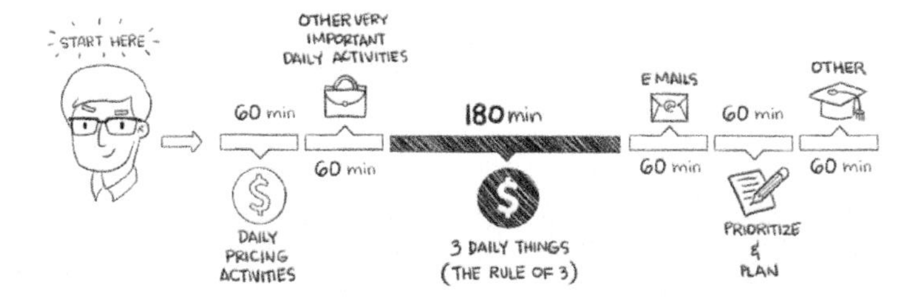

Finally, I recommend making sure you always have the right tools to make the most of the structure you've established for your day. One such tool that I recommend for top-of-the-class email productivity is Lean Mail. This tool gives you total control over your email. Using it, you will walk home with an empty inbox every day. I have found myself saving as many as two hours no longer performing pointless email activities on any given day thanks to Lean Mail (http://www.leanmail.com/).

How can I increase my average rates? (ADR)

"For every action, there is an equal and opposite reaction."

— Isaac Newton

This question can be answered with one simple rule, which goes like this: The only way to increase ADR is by doing things that do not lower it. This is probably not the answer you expected, but the best way to solve this problem is to inverse how you look at it.

Here is a good way to NOT lower your ADR.

The 20% Rule

What 20% of your business represents the highest-yielding ADRs? Figure out what business comprises this 20% and double down on your optimization directed specifically toward it.

Set action to what effects a big chunk of your business instead of directing your attention to everything. This will create momentum to increase your ADR.

Here are some thoughts on what to consider once you know what business to focus on.

Price & rate strategies

The paradox here is normally that if you increase rates you will receive less demand from these channels. If you receive less demand from you best ADR channels your ADR will decrease. Find ways to stimulate incremental business instead. To do this, consider the following:

Automation

Create automated rate restriction strategies. Set up a system that helps you set the best pricing restrictions. This will free up time so you can focus on the 20% Rule. Review your automatic pricing set-ups once a month and change them when and where it is necessary.

Price Points

How strong is the correlation between higher BAR rates and declining demand for your hotel? Make sure you are not missing crucial price points in your rate setup. See BAR section on page 44 for more details.

Reference Price and Prospect Theory

What we do not want is to create a reference price that is lower than it should be. The reference price is what the customer expects the price to be based on memories of past prices, prices set by brand leaders, related products or the way a price is presented.

If you discount a room to much, you might risk lowering your hotel reference price. Be careful how you restrict prices for example promotions. A simple way to increase your reference price could be to display your rooms differently. Start with the upgraded room type(s), followed by your standard room type(s). When displayed in reverse like this, a potential guest might see this as a savings instead of a loss. You should definitely conduct some experiments here to figure out what would work best in your particular circumstances.

Daniel Kahneman won a Nobel Prize in Economics for his work developing Prospect Theory. Prospect Theory states that people make decisions based on the potential value of losses and gains rather than the final outcome. In other words, loss hurts an individual more than the equivalent gain makes him or her feel good. Once you understand the behavioral aspects of human decision-making, the possibilities are endless.

The takeaway, if nothing else, is to never stop experimenting to figure out what works and what doesn't work.

Promotions: The 100 Rule

Make your current offers more appealing to potential guests by applying the 100 Rule. This rule states that when a product's price is greater than 100 (regardless of currency) use absolute value to market a discount. When the opposite is true—the price is less than 100—use a percentage to market a discount.

> Imagine a hotel room sells for $500 a night
> A 3-night stay = $1500
> Promotional Discount: 10% off a 3-night stay
> Absolute value = Save $150
> Percentage value = Save 10%
> Which one sounds more appealing to you, the absolute value discount or the percentage value discount? (Remember, the discount amount is the same.)

> Now imagine a bottle of wine sells for $40
> Promotional Discount: 10% off
> Absolute value = Save $4
> Percentage value = Save 10%
> Which one sounds more appealing to you now, the absolute value discount or the percentage discount?

The above examples of The 100 Rule demonstrate that how people perceive an offer depends on how it is framed. Something as simple as framing a promotion's value in absolute terms rather than as a percentage, or vice versa, brings psychology to bear on how people determine whether or not to make a purchase. Consider this rule the next time you set up a campaign or plan a promotion. If you want to read more about the 100 Rule and other cool concepts, I highly recommend the book *Contagious, How To Build Word Of Mouth In The Digital Age* by Jonah Berger.

*****

Obviously, there are many more ways to increase your ADR than just the examples I provided in this chapter, but I hope this gives you some additional inspiration and tools to begin tackling your specific ADR challenge.

How should I think strategically when pricing for a big event in the city?

We sometimes find that the demand in a city is higher than its supply of hotel rooms. We all have the temptation, then, to price our rooms just a little bit higher than normal—especially pushing our highest rate higher than we normally would—which is fine, and makes perfect sense from mathematical and logical viewpoints. However, we must still consider this decision wisely before making such a decision to raise prices. Let me quote something from Richard H. Taylor's book, *Misbehaving, The Making of Behavioral Economics:*

"I once asked the owner of a ski lodge why he didn't charge more during the Christmas-week holiday, when demand is at peak, and rooms have been booked nearly a year in advance. At first, he didn't answer my question. No one had ever asked him why the prices are so low during this period, when prices are at the highest, but once I explained that it was economics, he caught on and answered quickly. 'If you gouge them at Christmas, they won't come back in March.'"

That remains good advice for any business that is interested in building a loyal clientele base.

I likewise believe that it's very important for us to understand the value of our product, because if we charge more than what a guest actually thinks the value of our product is, the risk is they won't book with us again in the future. They will leave the hotel feeling that they paid a high price only because they had to get a room in the city regardless. The guest won't feel, however, that they actually paid a price equivalent to the value of the product they received. This "feeling" of theirs can return to haunt your hotel in various ways, including such guests writing negative reviews (especially regarding value-for-price), being unwilling to promote your hotel to others, and, of course, choosing to lodge elsewhere in the future.

Another thing to consider about charging a price that is too high compared with the actual value of the product received is that when guests pay a price they believe to be too high, even before arriving at your hotel, they tend to look for evidence that confirms their belief they are not getting the worth they paid a premium for. They will use this evidence against you, either in the form of complaints or negative reviews. On the opposite side of this equation, however, is that if you sell your rooms at a price point that matches the correct value of your product, you will turn this "tendency" around: guests will look for evidence that confirms their belief that they received a great value for their money.

We can't just make our decisions from a logical revenue manager's standpoint; we must also consider and understand the psychological standpoint of the other human beings partaking in these transactions.

What are some good tricks to increase my room sales profit margin?

"Sometimes the questions are complicated and the answers are simple."

– Dr. Seuss

This one is actually very easy. Print out a top-50 list of who/what contributes most to your room sales. Start from the top of the list and set up actions for how to increase profit margins for each distribution channel, corporate account and rate plan. The only difficulty here is in overcoming your own potential procrastination that prevents you from actually taking action on your actions points!

Imagine if your hotel has a distribution partner that contributes to 10% of all your room sales. What happens if you come up with something that could increase your margin by 1%. How much revenue is that? This is a no-brainer, but what can you actually change?

Suggested actions for improving room sales profit

Compensation negotiation

Come up with a good simulation that demonstrates how both parties (your hotel and your distribution partner) can profit from lowering commissions by a certain percentage. A potential way to frame this would be to offer a distribution partner more room availability in return for decreasing their commission.

More room types = More availability and choice

Make sure your biggest accounts have access to as many of your room types as possible on the hotel's landing page. This will generate higher ADRs for this account and thus higher profit.

More for less

Find channels with the best profit margin for your hotel; see if you can compromise your rate to stimulate more sales. If you do this right and proactively replace this rate with lower margin rates, it will help you to increase your overall profit margin.

Content and relevancy

There is an entire chapter devoted to just this topic because it is so extremely important.

What is the best way to make a room revenue forecast?

"The best way to predict the future is to create it"

— Abraham Lincoln

I strongly believe that a forecast should be used to identify both opportunities and challenges in time to take proper action. The best way to make a forecast really depends on what your goal is.

Three types of forecasts

The passive forecast

Follow all recommendations from your systems, and if nothing out of the ordinary happens, the projections you forecast will be passive ones. They might be very accurate, but they will not be optimized.

This approach is usually based on historical figures and a computer-calculated projection of the future. The problem with this approach is that you can only really rely on it for short-term forecasting. By that, I mean, it will only be accurate for roughly the next thirty days. During these thirty days, however, you can use this approach to forecast occupancy levels per day, which is a great and proven weapon for determining the best short-term pricing levels.

The political forecast

Our superiors are expecting some hypothetical, pre-defined forecast based on assumptions and guesses. When this situation arises, we must stick to this forecasting approach, and if we fail, we must find good excuses as to why our forecast went unrealized.

This is by far the worst way to create a prediction for the future. This forecast is usually created using a pre-determined result for the property, applying only minor adjustments. Often this type of forecast is made without even considering the actual status of what is driving the current levels of occupancy or where they need to be right now in order to make an accurate forecast.

The action-based, offensive forecast

This is the best way by far for approaching the challenge of making a good forecast. A combination of historical facts, current trends, ongoing actions and new actions meld to create an offensive, realistic forecast.

Here, we rely upon historical data, ongoing actions, current reservation trends and new action points to make a projected outcome based on action, not wishful thinking.

A hack to start using this approach to forecasting effectively is to understand your lead time. What kind of business is booked and at what point in time?

Gather data and additional forecasts

Set up a procedure to have the group-booking department and/or conference department create a three to six month forecasts for all groups. They should provide you with this forecast five to ten days before you create your own forecast. This should not be something big or time consuming for them to accomplish.

How big are the variations they predict based on their own experience and day-to-day relationship with group bookers? Do they predict that groups will cancel, change the number of rooms booked (either up or down), etc.?

Relying on this procedure to gather more data will create additional benefits. Before you know it, there will no longer be any groups remaining with questions marks! This forecast procedure also ensures that regular follow up with all groups is made.

Lead-time buckets

Let's divide your business into three buckets.

1. Base = for many hotels, this is their most important kind of business. A rule of thumb is that if you have a healthy base you can yield higher rates for your remaining rooms. Base business is normally lower paying groups, crew or transient early birds.
2. Fill up = corporate and other individuals booking fifteen to sixty days before they are scheduled to arrive.
3. Top up = the business you generate zero to fourteen days before arrival. To perform the best, here you need to have your base and fill up buckets working effectively.

Forecast Periods

The absolute best way is to make forecasts for an entire period both by the month, when it's done far in advance, and daily for the short term.

–30 days or more into the future, make forecasts a minimum of once a month.

–30 days or less, make forecasts every day.

Identify Bottlenecks and over performance

Do not look at the overall performance; you have to dissect your business to see if you are on track with budgeted performance and where it underperforms. You need to be able to answer: What is currently driving your pickup in occupancy for a particular period? Can you do anything to stimulate pickup in poorly performing customer segments or rate categories?

Action

Create actions where you see opportunities. Ask yourself, can I over perform in one segment to help compensate for loss in another?

Be sure to follow up on previous actions created last month. Are they working: yes or no? If not, you must quickly pivot in another direction.

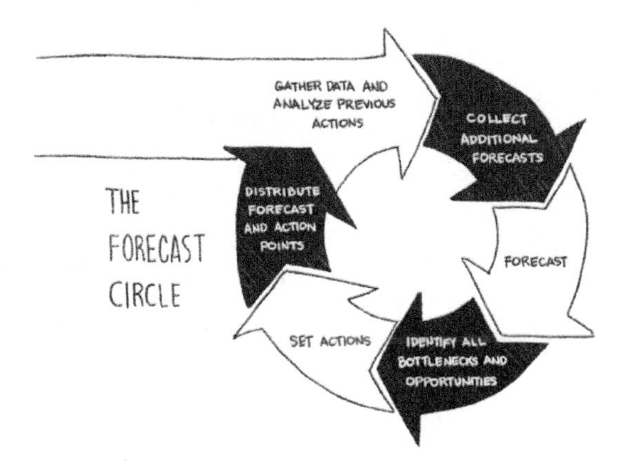

What are great tricks to generate more business during slow periods?

"Nobody wins unless everybody wins."

— Bruce Springsteen

The best way to avoid surprises when the quiet months arrive is to prepare well in advance. You do not ever want to be the cause of a price war that could potentially affect the whole market. Anything you do in public has a high risk of being detected by a competitor and copied. You must be smart and plan for the slow periods before they arrive.

Any market share you win by lowering your rate is just an illusion. When hotels lower rates on short before arrival, they only lower rates to the same people who had to travel to that destination anyway. This approach almost never creates incremental demand for the market. If you win market shares by lowering your rates for the short term, it will perhaps give you some gain in market share, most likely OPI (Occupancy). What happens in this situation, however, is that you end up selling cheaper rooms to the same demand rather than attracting new demand to the destination. The result is that the total pot of revenue is smaller, which eventually effects the RevPAR performance of the entire destination.

Here are some tricks on how to generate more business in both the long and short terms for slow periods. All actions qualify as non-pricing, which means that they do not necessarily affect your public rates. In other words, you do not have to discount or lower your public retail rates.

Long term

What has worked in the past?

Look at copy promotion and marketing actions from similar periods in the past. What normally drove your demand during these slow periods? Double down on your efforts there.

What specific markets book and how long before arrival do they book?

Run a few targeted campaigns. If you do not have access to such information, then ask some of your biggest OTA partners if they can provide you with the information you need.

Incentivize group reservations

Offer gift cards, freebies or other incentives to the person representing the company who actually makes the group reservation. For example, offer a voucher for a complimentary stay in the hotel suite. The group or group booker could give it as a prize at their next staff kick off.

Go all in when you create promotions

Do not create a promo, then just sit back and watch what happens. Use all available tools to stimulate as much demand as possible. Depending on which vendors you work with to publish your promos, see if they offer any additional tools that will give your promotions greater visibility. One such example is the *Travel ads* tool Expedia offers.

Travel ads gives you premium placement above the normal list of hotels. You do not pay an extra commission, instead you pay per click. I have tested this one with a very good return on investment. For example, the last *Travel ad* I used returned twenty-five times the amount of money invested in it.

Expedia's *Travel ads* also allows you to write your own headline and teaser text.

You can learn more about this tool at http://searchsolutions.expedia.com/

Bring back old business

This is a classic approach. Look at what groups and other business you had in the past and get the reservation's department to make cold calls to entice these groups and individuals to book again.

Customer Relationship Management (CRM)

If you have a modern CRM system, you could use your own database to customize the offers you make to your repeat business and most influential customers. Your most influential customers can, for example, be defined as those who have the largest social networks or are influential people within a large organization.

Call your 10 biggest distribution partners

Ask for their help. Normally this approach is very successful because, in addition to your receiving help, you give your partners authority and recognition. It can help you get your hands on something new and exclusive, whether it be a unique promotion for selected hotel partners or a new tool that can help you identify new opportunities. In other words, you never know what you might get just by asking.

Here are some examples:

1. Call Expedia and ask what they suggest for generating more business during the period when you need extra help. Ask them for their best advice and where you should focus your attention.

2. Ask your best wholesale partner if they have any opaque opportunities that you can get your hands on. Ask about potential campaigns or other high visibility actions.
3. Deal sites. This one is a bit controversial; either you love deal sites or you hate them. If they can bring you incremental business from markets outside of your own reach, I think they're a good thing. Do select them with care, however. Do not be afraid to test them out and form your own opinion, especially if they offer reasonable compensation levels.

Added value

How can you add value for some of your potential guests? E.g., if they book from you own website during a slow period, they could receive a free upgrade or another similar incentive.

Short term

Behind the scenes

Use channels without connections to metasearch engines. For example, use sites where guests must login to view your special offers. If you have access to such channels, try to do a last-minute campaign through one or more of them.

Corporate

Use your sales team to help incentivize customers or travel agents to book your hotel.

Public discounts and package discounts

If you have to create public discounts, to avoid price wars, use restrictions such as a minimum length of stay or a flash sale.

Another thing you could try is to make a special promotion on sites that package hotels with flights. Since your hotel is packaged with flights, your competitors will not see the promotion.

Upgrade promotions

Instead of lowering your price, create a discount for the type of room with the second-lowest price. This creates a compelling offer to potential guests, while at the same time it lowers the risk of being detected by competitors.

What are some good ways to improve my online content?

"A brand is no longer what we tell the consumer it is—it is what consumers tell each other it is."

– Scott Cook

It's said that content is king, but if that's true then context must be God. Make sure your content is persuasive and relevant. We have very little time to persuade the customer to choose our hotels over a competitor's.

A Microsoft study from 2014 shows that the human attention span has fallen from 12 seconds to 8 seconds from the year 2000—around the time the mobile revolution began—to 2014. The attention span of a goldfish is about 9 seconds. You have about 3 to 5 seconds to make an impression online.

With this in mind, consider how your hotel is displayed in these channels. Studies from www.reviewpro.com shows that top 3 reasons why a guest selects a hotel is:

1. Guest Experience Factors; i.e., Guest reviews and satisfaction scores
2. Location
3. Price

Do your landing pages and sell screens reflect these three reasons enough? Are they persuasive enough to convince potential guests to book rooms in your hotel? We have to play with the pictures in their heads, not simply what we think will work.

Use your own customer reputation tool or go to www.trustyou.com and search for your hotel. See what your guests place the most value upon. You cannot build on your weakness; you can only build on strength. Do your guests often give you praise for your great breakfast, your great location or how perfect your hotel is for couples? Make sure to include such strengths in your content on all your major channels. This is a great way to attract the perfect-fit guest for your hotel. Make sure the content is 100% optimized on all your different landing pages with them in mind.

Images

Experiment with the main images for your hotel and its rooms. Do not always follow the crowd. Remember, you have to stand out in the lists.

Studies and best practice materials from Expedia demonstrate that

- Travelers rank guest room images as the most important images to consider when booking a trip.
- 60% of travelers rank bathroom images as very important.
- Travelers are 150% more engaged on listings with more than 20 photos.
- Travelers want to be able to visualize where they are going to sleep, shower and relax after a busy day at work.
- Travelers prefer images that showcase your building in relation to the surrounding community. You can encourage them to imagine activities that are just outside your front door by including such images.
- Travelers look for bright lobbies with seating areas where they can relax or catch up on social media. Remember to showcase the public areas in your hotel.

- Food. How many images of food do you see on social media every single day? Food is social, indulgent and increasingly inspires travel. Include photos of your restaurant, bar, and room service so guests understand all of the opportunities to eat and drink available to them at your hotel. Be sure to highlight any unique experiences with food your guests will encounter, such as communal dining, access to space where guests can picnic, etc.

What are the most important yearly tasks for a revenue manager?

The most important yearly task, I think, is to create a realistic action budget. By action budget (or target), I mean a budget that is driven by commercial action points. You do not want to create a budget without first specifying the business mix you wish to achieve and how to reach those levels.

Budget

I believe there are two different types of budgets that reflect potential future outcomes.

1. The realistic action-driven budget
2. The realistic history-driven budget

You might ask, what is the problem if they are both *realistic*?

While your observation would be correct, note that the first budget is created using the following thinking:

> **How can we optimize what we have, learn by history and identify new opportunities to generate a realistic growth projection?**

While the second one is created out of the following thinking:

> **How can we leverage historical data and general demographic trends to create a realistic growth projection?**

The action-driven approach will always trump the history-driven approach. Both might be able to predict a realistic and nearly accurate outcome, but the action-driven approach will create new outcomes thanks to additional incremental growth opportunities, while the history-driven approach only creates organic growth.

The Action Budget

Ok, let us have a closer look at the action-driven budget approach.

A budget should not be something you make just once, then leave it. A budget should be a tool like any other tool you use all the time. The budget should preferably be divided into periods, and normally you would create one per each month of the year. Once you have defined your periods, it is time to look at the data.

Let us assume your budget should be divided into your different market segments or channels. Many times, you see that the budget is not broken down into anything other than some large buckets of different market segments or channels. It is very difficult to make an accurate projection based on large gatherings of data, which each behave very differently from one another.

Recommended data sets, information and tools to gather before you begin:

Expectations of the owner, brand or other stakeholders

What amount of growth is expected from your hotel?

Demand Calendar

Create a demand calendar for the entire calendar year. Identify potential demand using historical data, large group reservations and upcoming events.

Monthly business reviews from the previous year

What did you learn from similar periods last year? What can you fix, and what is worth repeating?

Relevant demographic trends

E.g., inbound travel behavior for a region and/or a country, macroeconomics and related industries.

On-the-books figures

What and how much do you already have on the books?

On-the-books period from last year

Compared with one year ago, are you ahead or behind?

Results from last year

What can we learn from last year, and how much can we expect based on that?

Market share (RGI, ARI and OPI)

This will help you understand how much potential for growth your hotel has during similar periods from year to year. Did you reach your fair share of the market last year? Where do we have the best chances to grow?

*****

When you have the above data sets, information and tools gathered, it is easy to identify where your biggest opportunities are. Ask yourself these questions to get started:

- Which segments have the biggest potential for growth, and what do we need to do to achieve this growth?
- How many new corporate accounts do you need to acquire to reach these new levels?

- What proactive approaches are needed to reach these new levels for group business?
- Do you need to plan specific promotions? When do you need to launch them? Etc.
- What is the average lead time associated with a specific growth segment? When and how can you start to measure progress to have enough time to pivot, if necessary, before it is too late?

Once your first draft is finished, it must be signed by the "owners" of each customer group. For example, make sure your sales manager is involved, and that he or she understands and acknowledges what must be done to reach the goals of the budget.

This is probably the most important step. The key to success is to make sure everyone involved knows what actions are needed to reach these levels. This is what will give you the momentum to reach levels you would not have reached otherwise.

BAR structure

The BAR (or Best Available Rate) is the lowest unqualified rate for a room type available to the general public. BAR provides a guarantee that guests will not find a lower rate for the same room type on a given night(s) on an OTA (or Online Travel Agent) or elsewhere. This is also a common rate used for rate comparisons between hotels.

I have found that the best way to optimize the BAR structure is to focus your efforts on the BAR levels that stand for 80% of your BAR traffic.

This is a great exercise to figure out what your "real" value is.

Let us say you have 10 BAR levels. See which of these levels bring you the most business at the moment; you should experiment by adding new levels or changing existing ones.

One important thing to remember is to also consider updating BAR to outside the 80% top business, but only the high ones. This might sound counterintuitive, but this is because many times you would have discounts connected to your BAR. When a discount is applied to a higher BAR, the final price for your consumer might be within the 80% span anyway.

Once you figure out what price points are selling the most, you'll also know where you should focus your efforts to make any necessary changes. By targeting the right price points, we can stimulate even more demand in the area that the crowd decided was your actual value.

In the figure below, we can see that 70% of all business is between price point 800 and price point 1,400. The most interesting part is that these price points come from only 30% of all the available price points illustrated in the graph. The second rectangle is also very important because the rates it represents are directly connected to that 70% of all business, since these price points are driving business for lower price points when discounted. In total, we see that 25% to 30% of all the price points represent 80% of the business in this example. If this were your hotel, it is here you would focus your attention.

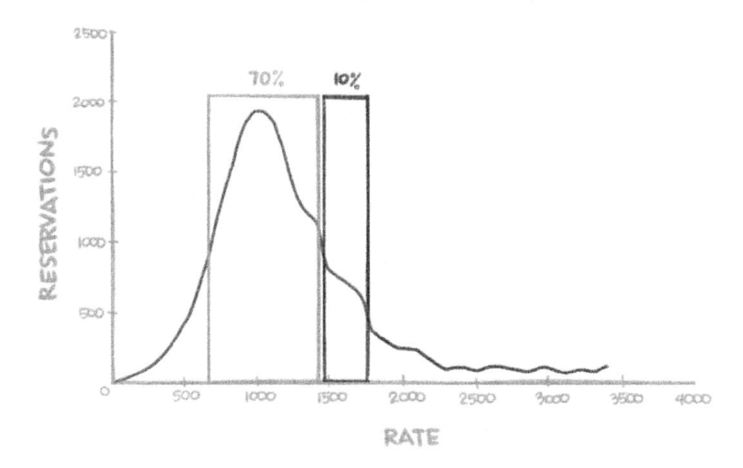

Create a scatter graph of price points for the business your hotel generates using the data on reservations that you downloaded from your system. If you do not know how to make a scatter graph, just Google it or go to YouTube and watch some videos, and you will become a master at graphing in no time.

This approach will help you gain insight as to where you should focus your efforts to create as much value as possible from your BAR structure.

Another great BAR exercise to do is to make sure your supplements make sense. How

much extra do you add for double occupancy, families, etc.? Make sure your rates make sense compared with your competitors and the market.

Flexible and nonrefundable BAR

Most hotels offer two types of BAR. Flexible rates typically mean that the reservation can be changed or cancelled until the day before arrival or sometimes until the same day as arrival. The other BAR type is a discount alternative where the customer must prepay. Reservations made with this rate type cannot be changed or cancelled. Thus, if a guest is willing to book early and commit to the reservation, some money can be saved. This means money in the bank for the hotel and a guarantee that the guest will arrive. Win-win for both parties.

One example of a successful nonrefundable setup is one where the hotel offers different levels of discount depending on how far in advance the guest is willing to book. This creates great search result relevance for hotels and at the same time more reservations long before arrival. It also gives a revenue manager extra tools to optimize the hotel revenue for the last remaining rooms because the base is already there.

Another advantage to catching early bookers is that they have a tendency to spend more money at the hotel since the memory of the purchase is further away when they arrive at the hotel than it is for somebody who booked a couple of days before arrival. In other words, this provides great prospects for upsell at arrival.

How can my hotel be *available* on all these strange websites with whom I have no direct agreement?

"The problem is not the problem; the problem is your attitude about the problem."

— Captain Jack Sparrow

First, let's look at what rates are actually available online. We can divide them into two different segments: qualified rates and unqualified rates. Qualified means that a potential guest in some way needs to qualify to be able to access the rate. Qualified could mean that in order to get a specific rate they need to also book a flight. The lower room rate is packaged with airfare. Unqualified means the rate is open to anybody. Good examples of unqualified rates are those rates a guest books on Booking.com or through your hotel's own website.

There are also plenty of websites with whom you do not have a direct contract that also offer unqualified rates for your hotel rooms. One example is www.agoda.com, while another is www.hotelsclick.com. These sites often display hotels with old or out-of-date content. From my own experience, customer service is also very poor with these sites.

These minor OTAs can cause severe headaches because they appear in the feeds of metasearch engines, this can cause additional minor headaches when:

- their rates are lower than those on your own website where you offer a best rate guarantee
- or your hotel's appearance is messy on the hotel-landing page within these search engines. The last thing we want to evoke from our customers is fear or doubt.

Ok, so why is it that OTAs are sometimes able to offer lower rates than the best available rates listed on your own website?

Leakage

There can be two major causes for what I will refer to as leakage.

Static Rates Leakage

Static rates leakage is the more common of the two. This leakage occurs when static net rates are distributed somewhere they should not be.

Allow me to oversimplify to make my point: possible scenario is that you have a NET/FIT rate agreement with a wholesaler. Let us assume this wholesaler has 1000 partners connected either directly through an interface or manually through a website. One of their partners distributes your room to another player who connects with a minor OTA. Normally you do not want your static rate to be available B2C without qualification because these rates are different from your normal retail rates. In other words, it should not be possible to book that rate unless they qualify for it the correct way. A publicly available website is not a correct way, unless it's packaged with a flight or something similar.

A correct way to sell or distribute a static rate would be, as mentioned, as part of a package, offline (through a travel agent), or within a closed environment. A closed environment could be a membership website for a credit card company with whom guests use your credit card member points to book hotel rooms.

Qualified Dynamic Rates Leakage

Let's say you have a OTA partner to whom you distribute your normal BAR and discounted rates. This could be one of the major OTAs. Here is another oversimplified scenario where this could go wrong:

You set up a promotion on one of your rates that has some restrictions attached to it. This restriction might be that the rate is only available to the South American market. One of the partners within their affiliate network somehow gets hold of the room rate (yes, they have big affiliate networks) and distributes the room to the domestic market in addition to the South American market.

*****

Above are just a few ways leakage can go wrong. This is very difficult to control and unlikely to go away anytime soon. Systems are only becoming increasingly connected; if we want to play within these segments, we must figure out the best structures to avoid as many issues as possible.

It's always very easy to blame somebody else for these issues when they occur, but first of all, we must realize that we are the ones responsible for making sure that we have a good setup in place before we start to find someone else to blame.

Tips and tricks

To finish answering this question, here are some rules and practical tactics for how to think about rate structures and content management.

Rule number one

The world is becoming increasingly connected. If you keep searching for ways to prevent your hotel rooms from being sold on OTAs where you don't have agreements, you will spend a lot of valuable time chasing ghosts. Instead, try to find opportunities within the problem.

Create a good strategy and setup for your rates. For example, if you want to prevent your rates from being sold at a lower rate as a result of leakage, make sure your setup ensures that if this happens it won't affect you that much, and the leakage will be easy for you to identify and take action against.

Again, it all comes down to lead times. Often, you see that these segments where you give static qualified rates normally have different lead times than your normal unqualified rates. If, for example, you see that most of these rates are being sold at least four weeks before arrival, the solution is simple: just set a high rate from the beginning for all the rates in this segment. This then allows you to offer a good early bird discount when rooms in this segment are booked far in advance. By doing this, you avoid having issues zero to thirty days before arrival when most people book online. This is a great way to control your distribution if you need or want to work with qualified static net rates.

Rule number two

Set up good check-in procedures at the hotel. If you have suspicions that a specific wholesaler or website is not obeying the rules that you established for them, be sure to collect reservation confirmation letters during check-in, as but one course of action. Then you can help yourself by helping your wholesale partner catch these crooks.

The first ring below represents a possible Qualified Dynamic Rates Leakage, while the next two rings represents possible Static Rates Leakage.

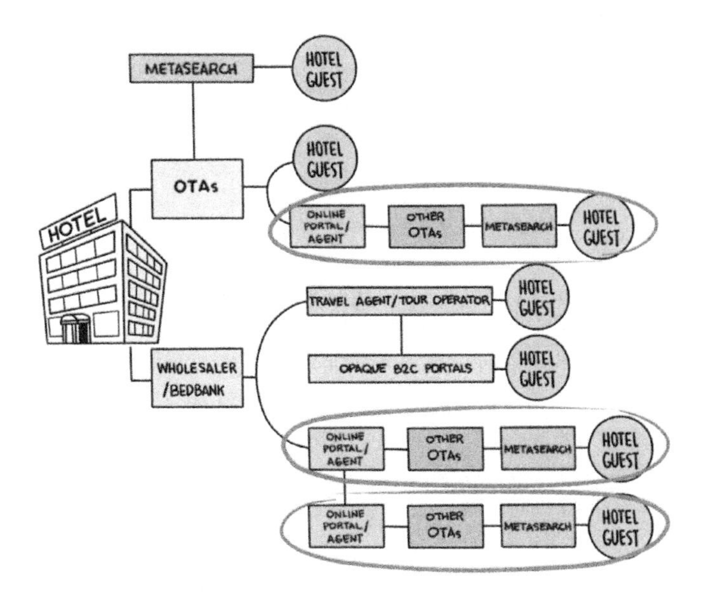

What are some practical tricks for group allocation and pricing?

"We learn little from victory, much from defeat."

— Japanese Proverb

If we start with allocation, I assume the questions are how to allocate groups and how much group business to accept on different dates, and so on. I believe that it is important to begin answering these questions by creating a demand calendar for the entire year. Normally, this is something you do well in advance. Create a demand calendar that indicates for every day of the year whether expected demand will be high or low, and, occasionally, even how much demand you can expect in terms of occupancy for each day.

Demand Calendar for groups

To explain demand calendars a bit more, I further believe it is good to indicate how much base business you would accept per day. By base business I mean groups, but also individuals booking far in advance. Once you define what base business is in your hotel and where you must draw the line for what you consider as base business or not, identify how much you're willing to accept per day during different seasons.

To perform this exercise, you obviously need to figure out what a healthy level of base business at your hotel looks like. By using historical data and looking at your different group segments, you will be able to determine what your historical levels of base business were and how much you're willing to accept for similar periods in the future. You also need to factor in events that will occur during the new period.

If you have access to systems with competitive intelligence, factor them in as well. This allows you to compare your own on-the-books situation with that of your competitors and/or the market as a whole.

Even if your high seasons are only a couple of months every year, and you don't see the point of creating a demand calendar for the entire year, specifying how much base business you're willing to take is, nevertheless, a great exercise to perform. Once you have a good calendar, it becomes a wonderful tool to pass out to other departments in the hotel, including those headed by the Front Office Manager and Reservation Manager, so they too can have a nice, simple overview. It also helps other employees to help you, allowing them to make many more decisions themselves without their needing to request your constant feedback.

One very important factor you need to consider while making this demand calendar is that you need to know what the wash rate is within different segments. Wash rate means how much of the initial group block did not materialize. For example, if a group blocks 100 rooms but cancels 30 of them within the contracted deadline, the wash rate for that group is 30%.

The wash rates often vary between segments and seasons. Leisure tour groups are more likely to wash than a business group.

Why do you need to know this? This is mainly because you probably want to sell more rooms than you have when you factor in wash rates. As an oversimplified example, if you set your base business contribution to be 30% on a given date and you know you will have at least a 50% wash rate, you should probably accept groups or other base business at a rate of up to 50 or 60%.

Group pricing

When it comes to group pricing, I want to discuss two different aspects of it. One aspect is displacement. The other regards what constitutes a good rate to offer a group.

Displacement requires that you determine how much business you must say "No" to if you accept a group. Basically, you need to look at what business you are expecting for the dates in question and whether the group replaces that business? You must also remember to add in extra revenues you would not have had otherwise with, for example, transient guests (conference rental, food, etc.).

To make these calculations, conduct a displacement analysis. You can either look at historical data or forecast performance with these specific dates in mind. Keep in mind that you don't always need to reinvent the wheel when you get a new group request necessitating that you make a displacement analysis. Take time to create a really good template you can use to make this a really simple procedure every time.

When it comes to group pricing, and assuming you don't already have an agreed upon rate with the hotel as a company or with a travel agent, figure out what would be the best rate to offer a group in order to win its business away from your competitors.

One great way to do this is to first look at the groups you did "win" in the past and see what rates you offered them in situations with similar circumstances. If, for example, in January last year you received a group request for a June booking for which you offered a room rate of one hundred euros per night, resulting in you winning that business, then it might be a good thing to offer a similar rate to another group request you receive in January of this year for June. It's also very important to look at the lead time of the request. In this example, a request received in January for a booking in June has a five-month lead time. However, if you receive the request in May for the June booking—a one-month lead time—then you probably want to offer a different rate.

When doing this exercise, be sure to factor in lead time and season. Make a habit of creating such a document with this data, that you can easily locate and reference when quoting rates to future groups. A similar exercise that inverts this process is to evaluate the groups you lost, rather than won. Determine at what rates you lose most groups for different lead times. I strongly suggest that you implement a system where you can—once a year or, preferably, once a month—evaluate all the lost business to see how you can approach rate setting differently in the future.

What Are the Best Ways to Deliver Professional Reports When Lacking Computer Skills?

"Acknowledging what you don't know is the drawing of wisdom."

— Charlie Munger

This is more normal than you think, but luckily, there is help available.

You can learn a great deal simply by taking online courses and watching YouTube videos. It doesn't matter if it's for Excel, PowerPoint or something else entirely. Invest some time in yourself. In addition to learning new computer skills, an added bonus is that taking this initiative will make you look good in front of your boss.

Remember, there are also websites where you can buy entire compilations of PowerPoint templates. As Pablo Picasso said: *"Good artists copy, great artists steal."*

Beyond learning computer skills related to specific software, there are also free revenue management courses available that you should look into.

Ways to invest in yourself

Below is a list of sources you can use to strengthen your computer and professional skills.

Class Central

This is a search engine for online courses (paid and free). You can browse subjects, search topics, or see trending courses.

www.class-central.com

Udemy

Twenty-four million students use Udemy, and they offer 80,000+ courses. This website is my personal favorite.

www.udemy.com

Coursera

Free online courses from top universities around the world. Their tagline is: "Build in-demand skills and earn valuable credentials."

www.coursera.com

edX

Take free online courses from the best universities and institutions in the world—Harvard, MIT, UC Berkeley, Microsoft, Tsinghua University, The Smithsonian, and more.

www.edx.org

Lynda

Paid membership gives you access to everything. Lynda is owned by LinkedIn.

www.lynda.com

YouTube

We all know YouTube. Most things you want to learn can be found here—free of charge.

www.youtube.com

Envato Market

Download cool PowerPoint templates here. This site offers ready-to-use design assets from more than 14,000 independent creators.

https://graphicriver.net/presentation-templates/powerpoint-templates

BONUS CHAPTER: What are some big trends coming up?

"I could either watch it happen or be part of it."

— Elon Musk

Writing this book in 2016, I believe there are five hot trends to keep your eye on.

Video

Video is here to stay and will soon become a very big part of how we view hotels online. By 2019, it is predicted that 80% of all Internet traffic will be videos. There are already established players out there helping hotels optimize for video. Travelclick is one such player. It's probably just a matter of time before the big OTA's tap into this golden opportunity.

Relevant advertising with simple user interfaces

One example is Facebook's Dynamic Ads and programmatic advertising. Programmatic advertising is all about relevance. We do not want to market to people who are not interested in travel or are not currently searching for hotels. With programmatic advertising, you can target people who searched for your destination or have booked a flight but have not yet booked their hotel. Think of it as relevant automatic marketing.

Advertising on Facebook and Instagram still remains much underpriced. Take advantage of this fantastic way to gain brand awareness and sell more rooms before it becomes Google expensive. New Facebook add-on features let you target people who have shown interest in specific destinations and travel dates.

Another company called Sojern can help you to programmatically target potential customers while they are visiting their favorite websites. This means, for example, that you could target a person who has booked a flight but did not yet book a hotel. Keep on giving them your ads until they book a hotel. If they book with another hotel, Sojern's programmatic advertising will know and stop sending ads to that person.

Niche booking applications

We all know that the major OTAs take pride in the fact that they have several hundred thousand hotels to offer their customers. However, this is a lot of content to provide to their customers in a clean and simple fashion that fits all.

In his book *Disrupt You*, Jay Samit writes:

"Anyone who's ever booked online knows that that most of the travel sites are difficult to use and aren't especially consumer-centric. The original OTAs based all of their booking systems on the same interfaces used by professional travel agents, rather than reimagining the process from a consumer's point of view.

"With so much content available, however, real challenge is no longer access to that content but discovery of it. Curation, collaborative filtering, and personalization are all paths for entrepreneurs to cash in on digital distribution without having to invest costly dollars in content creation. As Internet writer Clay Shirky points out, 'it's not content overload. It's filter failure.'"

We will see more and more personalized websites appear targeting specific niches of the market. Families, seniors, teens, millennials, etc. With all the content overload out there, the world is craving simplicity. Sites like Airbnb continue to inspire new ideas. The latest one is a website called Winston Club where you can find someone to share a hotel room with.

https://winstonclub.com/

As a Hospitality manger, we need to be aware of all new trends and figure out how we can become early adopters.

Messaging applications

Messaging applications such as Facebook Messenger and WhatsApp are the most preferred means of communication for millennials, but only the third most popular means among Generation Xers and the Baby Boomers.

In June 2016 Expedia launched a bot for Facebook Messenger called—you guessed it—Expedia bot, which does one thing, and does it well: it helps guests book hotel rooms. Using the chat feature, guests can enter parameters beginning with what city they would like to visit and the system will suggest hotels that meet those parameters. When guests complete their booking, they receive an updated message in the Messenger window with a link to their itinerary.

Slack is a popular messaging app for businesses. Slack is used to facilitate communications between teams and communities. Slack in known for its great connection with third-party apps such as Trello, Google Drive, Dropbox, Google Hangouts and Twitter. The app has a very rapid growth path with currently around two million active monthly users. Slack also already has a built-in travel booking service.

How can your revenue management strategy link with these technologies?

Facts

WhatsApp has 1 billion active monthly users

Facebook messenger has 900 million monthly active users

WeChat (China) has 650 million monthly active user

Big Data and CRM

Big data, this is a very trendy phrase, but what is it really?

Big data is a popular term used to describe the exponential growth and availability of data, both structured and unstructured. Another way to describe it is, big data is a large amount of data about people. Everything we do online leaves a trace. This data can help us to better understand behavior and, if structured in the right way, help us generate relevant information that we can use to our advantage.

One example is CRM (customer relationship management), which has evolved into reputation management. There is a large amount of data available about our guests and what they think of us freely available online in the form of reviews and profiles. CRM systems take all this data and puts it in a nice user interface for you to look at and, ultimately, base your decisions upon it.

Now CRM systems are also connecting to the popular revenue managements systems, which will include CRM KPIs in the decision-making algorithm. One such KPI is ReviewPro's GRI (Guest Review Index). I believe this index can help you gain a better perspective on how to price your hotel in comparison to a competitor's price. If your index is below 1.0 you would probably price yourself below your competitors, while if you're above 1.0 you could price yourself above them, since your perceived value is higher than theirs is.

Studies from Cornell University recently used GRI data to prove that a 1% increase in a hotel's GRI score results in higher profitability.

However, remember that what is most important is not a race to achieve data mastery but rather to formulate the right questions to ask, which is initially even more important than seeking the right answers. Once you know what these questions are, you can build your infrastructure based on them. If we do not know what to look for, the data alone cannot provide any answers.

GLOSSARY OF TERMS

Average Daily Rate (ADR) – A measure of the average room rate paid per rooms sold. To calculate ADR, divide room revenue by rooms sold.

Average Length of Stay (ALOS) – A measure of the total room nights in a hotel (or in a specific segment) per the number of total reservations in the hotel. To calculate ALOS, divide total occupied room nights by total bookings.

Average Rate Index (ARI) – A measure to determine whether the hotel realizes its fair share of ADR compared to a competitive set. To calculate ARI, divide the hotel's ADR by the ADR of a competitive set (that is representative of the market). An ARI equal to 1.00 indicates that the hotel has secured an equal share of revenue based on ADR compared to the competitive set. An ARI above 1.00 indicates a hotel has secured a greater share. An ARI below 1.00 indicates that the hotel has secured a lesser share. Multiply ARI by 100 or convert it to a percentage to ease the burden of working with this measurement.

Best Available Rate (BAR) – The lowest unqualified rate for a room type available to the general public. BAR provides a guarantee that guests will not find a lower rate for the same room type on a given night(s) on an OTA or elsewhere. This is also a common rate used for rate comparisons between hotels.

Booking curve – A tool that can visually represent bookings over time, incorporating data such as pickup, number of bookings, availability and yielding capacity of the hotel.

Booking window or Booking lead time – The time period between when a hotel reservation is made and a guest's actual arrival date. Measures how far in advance rooms are booked.

Block / Group pricing – A non-yieldable rate applied to a fixed number of rooms reserved for a specified group. A window exists during which members of the specified group must book their rooms in order to receive the non-yieldable rate.

Break-even – the point at which revenues equal costs.

Budget – Establishes a hotel's financial plan for the upcoming calendar or fiscal year. Generally, it should designate a daily occupancy, ADR and RevPAR for every major market segment. It outlines percentage changes over previous years, both by month and by quarter. This annual budget comprises part of the overall financial budget for the hotel.

Capacity – The number of rooms a hotel has to offer.

Central Reservation System (CRS) – A system to manage the booking process and existing reservations, and to maintain hotel information and data, including rates and inventory. Systems can either be created in-house or by a third-party vendor.

Channel management – The techniques and systems hotels use to update hotel information, room inventory and rates in each of their distribution channels.

Channels – The different means by which potential guests can reserve or book a hotel room.

Closed to arrival (CTA) – An inventory control mechanism used by revenue managers to prevent new reservations being made by guest arriving on a specific date. The only guests permitted to use such inventory are those arriving at earlier dates and remaining over the CTA date.

Cold / slow periods – A period of time (season, month, day, or time of day) when operating performance (demand) is low. Cold periods are times when revenue managers might discount rates or offer incentives in an attempt to increase occupancy and improve RevPAR.

Commission – The payment that a travel agent or other third party receives for each reservation made through their office or site.

Competitive set (or Compset) – Consists of a group of hotels recognized as direct competitors to the hotel by which the hotel can compare itself against the group's aggregate performance.

Conversion – The process of a guest moving from gathering information about a hotel or shopping for a room to taking action by making direct inquiries or finalizing a booking.

Conversion Rate (CR) – A statistical measure of the number of people who click an ad who eventually make a purchase associated with that ad. To calculate CR, divide the total number of buyers by the total number of unique clicks.

Cost Per Click (CPC) – The average cost to an advertiser incurred as a result of a consumer clicking an online ad.

Click Through Rate (CTR) – A measure of the total number of webpage impressions that result in clicks, representing the number of people who actually see an advertisement. To calculate CTR, divide the total number of clicks by the total number of unique impressions.

Demand – The amount of interest in a hotel, including in its beds, rooms, event spaces, etc.

Denial – A response to a potential guest's request stating that a hotel cannot accommodate any additional guests because it is fully booked or a restriction has been placed on the date requested.

Displacement Analysis – An analysis conducted to determine whether it's prudent to take rooms out of a hotel's inventory—usually to accommodate a group's request—that could be requested later at a higher rate by late-booking or walk-in guests. To conduct a displacement analysis, multiply the number of rooms denied by the average rate for that segment of business. If the resulting number is higher than the group revenue, then the group's request should be denied.

Dynamic pricing – A method hotels employ to help optimize profitability by changing prices for a room or service in response to changes in capacity, competition, demand and other guest attributes.

Elastic demand – When consumer demand responds to price changes. Factors that can influence elastic demand include increased competition, standardized services and perceived luxury.

Fenced rate – A rate that offers benefits to potential guests, but with conditions or requirements that apply in order to secure a reservation. To procure such a rate, reservations are often nonrefundable, purchased in advance and cannot be canceled.

Fixed pricing – A pricing strategy in which prices do not fluctuate based on demand, product characteristics or segmentation within markets.

Forecast – A prediction of the number of rooms that can be sold on a specific date or period of time. Accurate forecasting greatly enhances other revenue management strategies according to the expected level of demand.

Generic search – A search for a product in which the user does not enter a brand name as a keyword. When searching for a hotel, a user might type "downtown hotels in Boston," when seeking information about hotels in the Boston area, rather than specify a known hotel or chain.

Global Distribution Systems (GDS) – Four of the most recognized reservation systems in the industry: Amadeus, Galileo, Sabre and Worldspan.

Gross Operating Profit Per Available Room (GOPPAR) – A measure of total revenue less operational and marketing expenses per room used to measure a hotel's performance and to make adjustments accordingly. To calculate GOPPAR, subtract operational/marketing expenses per room from the total revenue brought in by rooms sold.

Group Displacement – A process of measuring a group's total profitability compared to the profitability of gaining business from other channels that would otherwise be displaced by the group.

Group forecasting – Making educated estimates for how many group block rooms will be booked and when, based on previous booking data.

Group Pricing – *See Block / Group Pricing*

Group segment mix – The proportions of the different group segments that comprise the total group business for the hotel. In general, these segments receive different rates.

Inelastic demand – When consumer demand does not respond to prices changes. Factors that can influence inelastic demand are reduced competition, differentiated services and consumer staples.

Landing page – The "front page" of a site a web user first arrives at as a result of clicking on a listing's link in a search.

Last room availability clause (LRA) – A contract clause—often agreed upon between the hotel and third-party agents—indicating that the contracted rate is available as long as rooms of any type remain available.

Leisure traveler – A traveler who travels for personal reasons rather than for work. Leisure travelers are not business travelers.

Length of stay – The number of nights a guest has booked at the hotel.

Length-of-stay controls – Controls put in place to help regulate demand for rooms in an effort to organize and optimize occupancy for a hotel.

Market Penetration Index (MPI) – A measure to help the hotel recognize its position in proportion to its competition by determining whether the hotel realizes its fair share of occupancy. To calculate MPI, divide the occupancy percentage of the hotel by the occupancy percentage of the competitive set (that is representative of the market). An MPI equal to 1.00 indicates that the hotel has secured an equal share of occupancy compared to the competitive set. An MPI above 1.00 indicates a hotel has secured a greater share of occupancy. An MPI below 1.00 indicates that the hotel has secured a lesser share of occupancy. Multiply MPI by 100 or convert it to a percentage to ease the burden of working with this measurement.

Metasearch engine – A website that can search all OTAs on behalf of a consumer and display the best available prices based on predefined criteria.

Net rate – The sell rate with commissions sometimes required by third-parties (namely, OTAs) already subtracted.

Occupancy – A measure of the percentage of available rooms sold during a specific period of time. To calculate occupancy, divide the number of rooms sold by rooms available.

Occupancy Index – A measure of the hotel's occupancy percentage compared to the occupancy percentage of the competitive set (that is representative of the market). To calculate the occupancy index, divide the hotel occupancy percentage by the occupancy percentage of the competitive set, then multiply by 100.

Online Travel Agency (OTA) – A web-based hotel and travel reservations system. Hotels offer inventory to OTAs, which sell rooms in exchange for a commission.

Opaque – Describes a booking channel that shields the identity of a hotel until a guest completes their reservation. It can also describe channels where guests must first become members to gain access to special rates.

Overbooking – A tactic of booking reservations beyond capacity to offset cancelled reservations and no-shows.

Pace – *See Pickup*

Pay Per Click (PPC) – An Internet advertising model where advertisers use ad links to direct traffic from host websites to their own websites or products. Advertisers pay the owners of host websites a fee each time an ad of theirs is clicked.

Perishable inventory – Inventory, that if not used within a specific period of time, becomes a lost revenue opportunity. A hotel room is perishable inventory.

Pickup / Pace – The rate at which reservations are booked for a specific date.

Price Elasticity – A measure showing how demand for a room responds to a change in its price.

Property Management System (PMS) – A hotel's onsite system that facilitates management processes for the hotel, including guest check-in and check-out.

Rate parity – A guarantee that potential guests will be quoted the same price for the same product regardless of where they shop. It allows individual hotels and chains to set the same price for each of their room types across all distribution channels.

Reference price – The price consumers think a service, product or room should cost. Points of reference for prices include the price last paid, the price most frequently paid, the price other consumers have paid for the same thing, or market prices and posted prices.

Regression – A statistical analysis for evaluating the relationships that exist among variables. It measures the association between one variable (the dependent variable) and one or more other variables (the independent variables), usually formulated in an equation.

Reputation management – Influencing and controlling an individual's or business's reputation, particularly as it appears online or through social media.

Revenue Generating Index (RGI) – *See RevPAR Index (RPI)*

Revenue Management – The art and science of predicting real-time customer demand and optimizing the price and availability of products to match that demand.

RevPAR Index (RPI) – A measure to determine whether the hotel realizes its fair share of revenue compared to a competitive set. To calculate RPI, divide the RevPAR of the hotel by the RevPAR of the competitive set (that is representative of the market). An RPI equal to 1.00 indicates that the hotel has secured its fair share of revenue compared to hotels it the competitive set. An RPI above 1.00 indicates the hotel has secured a greater share. An RPI below 1.00 indicates that the hotel has secured a lesser share. Multiply RPI by 100 or convert it to a percentage to ease the burden of working with this measurement.

RevPATI – Revenue per available time-based inventory unit. RevPAR and RevPASH are variations on this measure. RevPATI is calculated differently depending on the context. It is used in all applications of revenue management to analyze a hotel's or chain's ability to optimize its revenue capacity.

Revenue per available room (RevPAR) – A measure of how well a hotel manages its inventory and rates in order to optimize revenue. To calculate, multiply occupancy by ADR.

Search engine optimization (SEO) – The process of maximizing unique visitors to a website by improving the site's position in organic search results.

Segmented markets – Markets composed of consumers bearing similar characteristics. Segments can be comprised based on consumers' ages, purchasing power, frequency of purchase, and affiliation to groups; or be differentiated by how much they are willing to pay for a service, product or room.

Shoulder Date – Dates that fall directly beside or very close to other high demand dates. A Friday and a Sunday are each considered shoulder dates when they are not sold out, but the Saturday between them is.

Stay Pattern Management – The process or optimizing hotel capacity by ensuring the stay patterns on the books do not result in unsellable stay patterns remaining to be booked.

Time-variable demand – Uncertain demand that varies by time of year, day of week, in relation to holidays, etc.

Transient – Non-group or non-committed business (guests). These guests are largely on-the-move and seeking short stays.

Unconstrained Demand – A forecast of the quantity of rooms a hotel could sell if had an unlimited number of rooms—that is, no constraints or limits.

Variable pricing – Simultaneously offering varying prices at different points-of-sale (including websites) for the same service, product or room.

Wash – The fraction of the group block that the group does not utilize.

Win rates – The rate at which potential guests accept offers.

Worldspan – GDS system originally designed for airlines, now widely used by travel agents to book all forms of travel.

Yield – Revenue made. Includes the dynamic pricing, overbooking and allocation of perishable assets necessary to maximize revenue.

Yield Management – Synonymous with Revenue Management, the purpose of Yield Management is to maximize revenue and profits. The process involves understanding, anticipating and reacting to guests' needs and behavior, with the intention of increasing yield.

Printed in Great Britain
by Amazon